SEVEN SECRETS
FOR KICKING THE HABIT
A Holistic Approach to Getting Your Addictions Under Control

by H. David Schuringa

CBI Publishing Center
PO Box 900
Grand Rapids, MI 49509-0900
www.cbi.tv

ISBN: 978-1-4675-7695-6

TABLE OF CONTENTS

INTRODUCTION

Countless millions wrestle with one or more addictions, and so countless books have been written on the subject. Why one more?

Sobriety is a journey. Many do not know the secrets of a successful journey, one that will lead to serenity. This book provides a unique approach.

You will see in this book a commitment to a holistic approach. That is why chapter 3 contains an invitation to deep spiritual renewal; chapter 4, to a thorough renewing of the mind; and the following chapters, to the strengthening of our resolve to do what we know needs to be done.

The first two chapters tackle issues foundational to kicking the habit: recognizing denial and the practical implications of the sometimes heated debate about whether addiction is a sin or sickness.

I hope that this book will be helpful because it is relatively brief and highly practical. It is important to me, as a practical theologian, to bring theological theory into everyday praxis (practice or action) in a way that empowers regular folks to actually benefit from it. You do not have to slog through hundreds of pages for a couple sips of help. Every page in this short book is worth gold and will be helpful to you.

Drink deeply.

In short, I believe that my commitment to practical theology, along with my experience successfully counseling addicts of all kinds, makes this book a unique contribution to the field.

At the end of the book, you will find a study guide for each chapter to complete as you are reading. This makes the book adaptable for individual or group study. The guide will enhance your study by providing a way to process the material.

As you discover the seven secrets for kicking the habit, may you embark on a journey to a new life—one that is free and splendid. After all, that is how life in Christ is supposed to be.

SECRET 1

ADMIT THAT YOU ARE AN ADDICT

SECRET 1

ADMIT THAT YOU ARE AN ADDICT

Test me, Lord, and try me, examine
my heart and my mind.
–Psalm 26:2

A drunk walks into a bar, sits down and demands a drink. "Get out," says the bartender. "I don't serve drunks here." The drunk staggers out the front door, only to come back in through the side door. He sits at the bar, bangs his fist and demands a drink. Indignant, the bartender responds, "I just told you to get out, didn't I? NOW LEAVE!"

The drunk gets off his stool, stumbles out the side door and comes back inside through the back door. Once again, he sits at the bar and loudly asks for a drink. The bartender, now glowering, looks at the drunk and yells, "I TOLD YOU, NO DRUNKS ALLOWED! NOW GET OUT!"

The drunk looks up at the bartender and slurs, "How many bars do you work at, anyway?"

THE MANY FACES OF ADDICTION
Funny? Perhaps, but we don't find these jokes as hu-

morous as we used to. That is because we now know more than ever that an addiction is serious business, a condition that quickly becomes an epicenter of distress and dysfunction.

No addiction is a laughing matter.

All kinds of behaviors can become addictions. The ones we hear about most are drugs, alcohol, gambling and tobacco. But there are other behaviors to which you can become addicted, such as eating food, looking at porn, playing video games and even jogging or shopping, to name a few.

As we will see, addictions are not a big mystery. In fact, whatever faces addictions take on, they are all basically the same. Whether we are talking about the cause or the cure for addictions, if you understand one, you pretty much understand them all.

But how do you know if you have an addiction?

> If you know how to deal with one addiction, you pretty much know how to deal with them all.

It is not difficult to find screening tests for alcohol or drug addictions. We have included one for your convenience in appendix 2. Tests such as this can be adapted to any type of addiction, whatever it looks like.

However, the problem with such tests is that they often provide you with little more than the *probability* that you or a loved one is an addict. When you are dealing with low or even high probabilities, there is too much wiggle room. You can conclude, "No, I don't think I have a problem after all."

THE DEFINITION OF ADDICTION

How can you know for sure if you are an addict? For some of you, that may seem like a dumb question—anyone can see that you are hooked. But the fact is that you often become an addict well before it becomes so painfully obvious to those around you.

To determine whether you are an addict, first we need to define addiction.

An addiction is a repeated behavior that has become a habit and that you continue in spite of its negative effect on your life.

Let's break this down.

A repeated behavior: You don't just do it once or twice; rather, you do it again and again. For example, perhaps a couple of times in your life you had too much to drink—maybe you even got stone drunk. That alone does not make you an alcoholic. You sinned by drinking too much, and you know the Bible frowns on drunkenness (Ephesians 5:18). But it was a one-time deal. Everyone makes mistakes. If you continue engaging in that behavior over and over again, however, there is cause for concern.

15

...that has become a habit: A habit is "an acquired behavior pattern regularly followed until it has become almost involuntary."[1] In other words, the repeated behavior has become ingrained in your lifestyle.

This does not necessarily mean that you repeat the behavior several times a day, or even every day. You can have a habit of buying a handful of lottery tickets or going down to the casino only once a week—say, every Friday night after you receive your paycheck. I once heard of a teacher who didn't drink during the entire school year, but when summer hit, she would go on a two-month binge. Every year.

These are habits.

A habit is a predictable pattern of behavior that has developed and is maintained, regardless of frequency.

...and that you continue in spite of its negative effect on your life: There are good habits and bad habits. Being kind, reading your Bible and brushing your teeth are good habits. Bad habits are, well, bad for you. They have, or will have, negative consequences that affect your body, your family, your job or some other area of your life—if not all of the above.

So what does addiction look like? At first, you repeat a harmful or potentially harmful behavior. Then, it becomes a habit. Finally, it begins to damage your life, and it probably harms the lives of those around you.

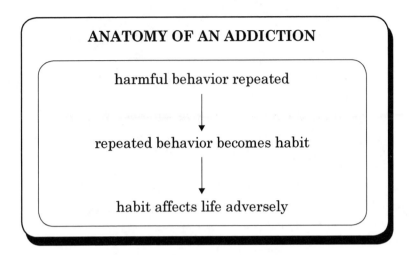

ANATOMY OF AN ADDICTION

harmful behavior repeated

↓

repeated behavior becomes habit

↓

habit affects life adversely

OWNING UP TO THE DAMAGE

"Hi, I'm Bob, and I'm an alcoholic" is the familiar re-frain from Alcoholics Anonymous meetings. There is some debate about whether people should consider themselves addicts for the rest of their lives, even after they have stopped drinking, but no one would negate the importance of recognizing that a person is an addict when his or her life is spinning out of control.

Here are some examples:

> A drug addict keeps using, even though he is breaking the law and the habit is costing him his job and family.
> An alcoholic will not stop drinking, even if her liver is as big as a house, she has earned a DUI or she is causing brain damage to her unborn child.
> A smoker keeps lighting up, no matter how much a pack costs and regardless of the fact that the

secondhand smoke is choking everyone within reach.

> A food addict keeps sneaking back to the buffet until she drops dead of a heart attack.
> A porn addict can't get enough smut and rarely gives a thought to his betrayal of his current or future wife.
> A shopaholic becomes oblivious to enormous credit card debt, as well as to the bags of unopened purchases scattered around the house.

You get the idea: addiction is a habit creating harm.

The first secret for success in overcoming an addiction is examining your life (and being open to someone who cares for you helping you examine your life objectively) and then admitting that you are an addict—that a certain habit is causing problems. At this point, you need to look in the mirror and say, "I'm Bob, and I'm an addict."

DENIAL AIN'T NO RIVER IN EGYPT

There is no denying that admitting that you're an addict is excruciatingly difficult. It requires painful honesty. What makes it even more difficult is that by the time the addiction has taken charge, it has brainwashed just about every aspect of your being into denying that there is anything wrong or that you are out of control.

This is called "denial."

Denial is a defense mechanism "in which a person is faced with a fact that is too uncomfortable to accept and rejects it instead, insisting that it is not true despite what may be overwhelming evidence."[2]

Indeed, it is not atypical for addicts to refuse to accept their condition even in the face of "overwhelming evidence."

As they say, "Denial ain't no river in Egypt." It is the primary culprit blocking you from recognizing that you have a problem, especially if your life has not yet hit bottom and you are still functioning reasonably well.

Proverbs 23:29–35 describes a drunkard in unflattering terms:

> Who has woe? Who has sorrow?
> Who has strife? Who has complaints?
> Who has needless bruises? Who has bloodshot eyes?
> Those who linger over wine,
> who go to sample bowls of mixed wine.
> Do not gaze at wine when it is red,
> when it sparkles in the cup,
> when it goes down smoothly!
> In the end it bites like a snake
> and poisons like a viper.
> Your eyes will see strange sights,
> and your mind will imagine confusing things.
> You will be like one sleeping on the high seas,
> lying on top of the rigging.

"They hit me," you will say, "but I'm not hurt!
They beat me, but I don't feel it!
When will I wake up
so I can find another drink?"

You may be tempted to think, "Well, until I look like this, I am not an addict." The trouble is, however, that the pathetic figure in the proverb might not be an addict at all! He might be simply a drunkard. You, on the other hand, may be an addict even though at this point your life appears "normal" and you are not sleeping in a homeless shelter.

When it comes to alcohol addiction, we refer to someone who doesn't look like the guy in the gutter as a "functioning alcoholic." Unfortunately, when you appear to be at the top of your game, denial can settle in all the more firmly as your life, perhaps slowly and subtly, slides into dysfunction.

But whether you have reached bottom, are hitting a few bumps in the road or are a functioning addict, it is possible to stop the slide and to reverse your course. There is a road to success that, by God's grace and with the help of this book, you can travel. The **first secret** of kicking the habit and beginning that journey to serenity is admitting that you've got a problem.

KEY IDEAS FROM CHAPTER 1

> All addictions are basically alike, and they are not a mystery.

> An addiction is a repeated behavior that has become a habit and that you continue in spite of its negative effect on your life.

> Owning up to the damage your addiction causes is the first secret of recovery.

> "Denial ain't no river in Egypt."

> It is highly possible to be a functioning alcoholic—to have a problem and yet not be the drunkard who is the butt of jokes.

SECRET 2
RECOGNIZE THAT YOU ARE SICK AND SINFUL

SECRET 2

RECOGNIZE THAT YOU ARE SICK AND SINFUL

[He] forgives all your sins and heals all your diseases.
–Psalm 103:3

The moderator pounded the gavel on the desk and cleared his throat. "Ahem. Welcome to Point-Counter-Point. Our special guests today are Dr. Will Powers and Dr. Kent Helpit. Why don't we begin this little chat?"

He said "little" because he knew the discussion would not get very far. "Dr. Powers, would you care to begin?" Dr. Powers jumped right in.

"I'm sick of hearing all this nonsense about addiction being a sickness. Ridiculous! The fact that someone is hooked on alcohol or drugs, or anything else, is merely a matter of having made wrong moral choices. To correct the situation, that person needs to start making right moral choices. Just say no, for crying out loud! You loonies in the therapeutic ring do a lot of damage by absolving people of their personal responsibility."

At the end of his speech, Dr. Powers crossed his arms

and stared his opponent down with a "Go ahead, make my day!" kind of look.

Dr. Kent Helpit took a sip of water, adjusted the spectacles at the end of his nose and began to make his case.

"Well, that's easier said than done, my dear Dr. Powers. Better men than us have tried to quit by sheer force of will but have found it utterly impossible. The disease theory indicates that something is very wrong physically (and probably genetically) and that the body of an addict just does not process, say, alcohol the way 'normal' folks do. It is poison for addicts. And it is decidedly not their fault that they are like this and in need of help."

"You legalistic willpower folks," he continued, "are doing insurmountable damage by loading guilt on people by the shovel full and sidestepping the real issues. In fact, your guilt makes things worse, causing addicts to drink even more. We, however, provide hope and help that can lead to their healing."

At this point, Dr. Will Powers stormed off the set. End of "discussion," apparently. The moderator cut to a commercial.

THE SIN SCHOOL
There are two primary schools of thought on the nature of addiction, and, as in our chat with Dr. Will Powers and Dr. Kent Helpit, the schools appear diametrically opposed. They appear, in fact, as different as night and

day. We will call these two schools "the sin school" and "the sickness school."

Those from the sin school tend to hold to either the deliverance or nouthetic model, both of which see alcoholism, for example, as simply a matter of immoral behavior—sin—that an individual needs to quit.

The deliverance model sees this as happening with the aid of a dramatic event, such as a faith healing, brought about by the Holy Spirit. This event is almost like a second conversion in which a person experiences a sudden, tremendous change. The addiction is abandoned all at once, instantaneously—rather than gradually, over time.

The nouthetic model[3] sees overcoming addiction as a matter of exercising one's sanctified willpower by putting off the old person and putting on the new. Both models are saying essentially the same thing: addiction is a sin that you need to stop, and you can.

The sin school considers the sickness school wrongheaded. After all, if you think of addiction as merely a sickness, you are abdicating your personal responsibility, aren't you? In fact, an addict could just say, "I can't help it. I'm sick!" By this line of reasoning, just as you can't help it if you catch the flu, you can't help it if you catch alcoholism. Moreover, you need an expert to heal you.

The sin school will have none of this. Especially Christians, it asserts, ought to own up to their sin and acknowledge that they have done wrong instead of hiding behind the skirts of a supposed sickness. Christians, as new creatures in Christ, have the ability to stop sinning, and they must.

THE SICKNESS SCHOOL

In the sickness school are the medical and the twelve-step models, which see addiction primarily in terms of disease. Also known as the disease model, the sickness school understands addiction as a crippling dysfunction of major, and fairly complicated, proportions.

In contrast with the sin school, the sickness school holds that addicts obviously do not have the power to quit. This school holds up as an example the alcoholic who says, "It's easy to quit. I've done it dozens of times."

Rather than assess guilt or blame, the sickness school urges addicts to admit that they are in fact powerless in the face of their addiction and desperately in need of help.

What is the nature of this sickness? The sickness school holds that there are physical, probably genetic flaws that give someone a predisposition toward addiction. The sickness school holds that such a predisposition is not an excuse to drink any more than a person's allergy to fish is an excuse to eat fish. Both are "sick," and this concept of sickness provides a larger framework for understanding addiction.

According to the sickness school, medicine may indeed be needed to assist in withdrawal. Certainly, the addiction has damaged the brain and body of the addict, in many cases requiring further medical assistance of some kind. A doctor will prescribe a healthy diet, exercise, a vitamin regimen and a positive lifestyle. There may also be medications (e.g., an antidepressant drug) prescribed to assist in the withdrawal and to balance a flawed system.

The sickness school tends to consider the sin school naïve and simplistic. It holds that the sin school not only overestimates an addict's (flawed) willpower but also grossly underestimates the varied and profound effects of addiction upon a person.

THE WHOLE PERSON SCHOOL

So who is right? Is addiction a matter of sin or sickness? Actually, there is a third way, which we will call "the whole person school."

Today, theologians and scholars in the field agree that both the sin and sickness schools of thought make vital contributions to our understanding of addiction.

Of course addiction involves sin. When we engage in behavior that is harmful to us and to others, it is morally wrong. And no one feels more guilt for sin than an addict. But addicts often attempt to soothe their overwhelming guilt by intensifying the addiction.

It is worth noting that some addictive behaviors are sinful in and of themselves, while others are not. Pornography and the use of illegal drugs are inherently sinful behaviors, *and the goal should be complete cessation.* However, Christians are divided as to the sinfulness of a moderate use of alcohol or tobacco. I think gambling is a sinful lack of stewardship, but others would disagree, saying that even starting a business is a gamble. If a person is addicted to food or shopping, he or she can't stop eating forever or never shop again. These addicts have abused something that is good in and of itself *and need to bring their addiction under control.*

Rather than turning to an addiction to numb our conscience, we must repent and acknowledge that we need God to help us. We must make amends to those we have wronged. We must start on a path of spiritual renewal. And we can do these things through Christ who strengthens us (Philippians 4:13).

I love the old Johnny Cash song "I Came to Believe." In it, Johnny describes how hard he tried to solve his own problems—and how impossible that was. It is only when we turn matters over to God that we can find hope and healing.

But addiction is not simply a spiritual problem. It also involves disease, and any addict knows deep down that he or she is a very sick person.

The addict has a moral obligation to get help for healing, as does any sick person, if he or she is able. If we do have a physical or genetic disposition toward addiction, we need to learn to avoid that which may be poisonous to our system.

We may need medical help to repair any damage the addiction has caused. We need to find a recovery program that is right for us in order to remain free from the addiction and to bring healing and wholeness to mind and body.

THE WHOLE PERSON SCHOOL

Sin School	Sickness School
Deliverance Model	Medical Model
Nouthetic Model	Twelve-Step Model

TWO SIDES OF THE SAME COIN

So the huge chasm between the sin and sickness schools is not as wide as it appears at first glance. When seen through the prism of the whole person school, the sin versus sickness debate is clearly a false dilemma.

The **second secret** of kicking the habit is coming to understand that as an addict you are both sick and sinful. On your journey to sobriety, you will need both forgiveness and healing. The sin and sickness schools happen to be two sides of the same coin. You need to invest the whole coin to overcome addiction in our fallen world.

Dr. Will Powers and Dr. Kent Helpit need to keep talking. When you understand the true nature of addiction and how it affects the whole person, you will be pointed in the right direction—toward hope and healing.

KEY IDEAS FROM CHAPTER 2

> The sin school says that addiction is nothing more than a moral choice.

> The sickness school says that addiction is a sickness from which a person needs to be healed.

> The whole person school says that addiction involves both sin and sickness.

> On your journey to serenity, you will need both forgiveness and healing.

> Only by treating the whole person in Christ can someone get on the road to success.

SECRET 3
START WITH THE HEART

SECRET 3

S T A R T   W I T H   T H E   H E A R T

My heart rejoices in the Lord...
for I delight in your deliverance.
–1 Samuel 2:1

Ashley and her husband came to me after class. I was lecturing at a nearby college and had closed by sharing about Crossroad's prison ministry. She wanted to tell me that she was a returning citizen.

"Growing up, I couldn't understand why I was always so angry. I felt empty inside, and I was constantly burning with rage. I experimented with alcohol, drugs and sex to make the bad feelings go away. But what finally did the trick was robbing convenience stores with my friends. What a rush! It wasn't for the money or the products, just for the thrill. Until the night we got caught."

"Did you have a father growing up?" I asked.

"No," she responded. "But in prison I discovered that I have a heavenly Father who, in Christ, loves me deeply and will never abandon me. When I encountered him, the emptiness and anger disappeared."

THE HOLE IN YOUR HEART

Addiction attempts to fill a void inside that only God can fill. This "God space" in our hearts becomes an aching hole. Any number of things could have created the void: childhood abuse or neglect (as in Ashley's case), poor role models, habitual sin or simply the hard knocks and disappointments of life. In fact, we are flawed from birth, so in a sense each one of us was born with a hole in our heart.

Addictive behavior seems to fill the void and temporarily relieve the pain. It feels good, and that is

> Any number of things could have created that hole in your heart.

why we keep going back to it. It is no wonder that drugs were frequently involved in pagan religious ceremonies. The euphoric high made participants feel close to the gods.

The famous psychologist Sigmund Freud, though remarkably intelligent, used cocaine for years to find relief from bouts of depression and anxiety. "A small dose," he wrote, "lifted me to the heights in a wonderful fashion. I am just now busy collecting the literature"—in German, French and English—"for a song of praise to this magical substance."

This is one of the reasons that beating an addiction is such a challenge. Have you ever seen someone on methamphetamine? I am not proud to confess that one of the reasons I stayed away from drugs in college is that, having seen other students partake, I was afraid that once

I started, it would feel so good that I would never want to stop!

Addictions reach down into the deepest levels of our inner being, deep down into our God space. It feels like magic, like a miracle, like eternal bliss—for a while.

HE IS KNOCKING ON THE DOOR

However, the truth of the matter is that an addiction, no matter how good it feels, soon begins to cause more problems than it "solves."

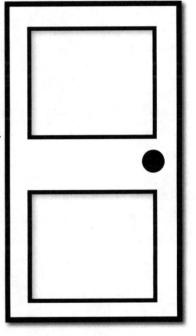

The magic goes up in smoke. The miracle is exposed as a fake. The eternal bliss becomes a sort of hell. We can go from addiction to addiction searching for that elusive feeling, but ultimately the search will fail. Slowly but surely, almost imperceptibly, the addiction takes the place of the real deal: the intimate relationship with God for which we were created and redeemed.

Even for sincere Christians, overcoming addiction requires a conversion of sorts. We need to invite Jesus into our hearts as he knocks on the door. He won't break the door down. He is waiting for you to answer it.

On Easter Sunday evening, Jesus was on the front porch of the people he had met on the road to Emmaus. Dr. Luke reports that Jesus "continued on as if he were going farther" until they urged him to enter (Luke 24:28–29). Jesus wasn't "faking it"; he was eliciting their invitation.

So too we must open the door of our heart and invite him in: "Here I am! I stand at the door and knock. If anyone hears my voice and opens the door, I will come in and eat with that person, and they with me" (Revelation 3:20).

He is knocking, and his knock is irresistible. I mean, how long can you leave Jesus standing on the porch and refuse to open the door?

Similarly, the Heidelberg Catechism says, "God gives his grace and Holy Spirit only to those who pray continually and groan inwardly, asking God for these gifts and thanking him for them."

Deep down, you do not long for a drink or a joint—you long for a sip of living water (John 4:10). Only Jesus can bring *everlasting* satisfaction.

Inviting Jesus into the home of our hearts involves not only extending the invitation but also confessing sin, making amends with those we have wronged and nurturing a robust devotional life as we deepen our relationship with God. We must clear the junk out of our

God space to make room for Jesus.

DEEPENING YOUR LIFE WITH CHRIST
When Daniel was a prisoner in Babylon, he committed himself to personal devotions three times a day. Crossroad students receive Straightway Roadmaps that are designed to help them read Scripture devotionally while they await the arrival of their next lesson. The corrected lessons and Instructor letters that students receive are intended for devotional review. We hear that they study these resources again and again.

There are other daily helps that you may enjoy, such as *Morning and Evening* by Charles Spurgeon, *Our Daily Bread* from RBC Ministries and *Today* devotionals from Back to God Ministries International. Regardless of the materials you use, you want to nurture a warm, personal and deep relationship with Jesus, your friend, who satisfies far more than the fleeting pleasure of addictions can.

In addition to studying the Bible and praying, enter God's presence with singing and praise (Psalm 100:4). The Bible teaches that God himself is enthroned upon the praises of his people (Psalm 22:3). You might not be able to sing out loud very often in your current situation, but you can offer praise in your heart or just listen for God's singing over you (Zephaniah 3:17).

A historical, biblical practice that seems to have all but disappeared is spiritual meditation. Meditation involves thinking deeply about, mulling over, pondering and reviewing matters of the faith, doctrine and especially Christ.

As Puritan Edmund Calamy wrote, "A true meditation is when a man doth so meditate of Christ as to get his *heart* inflamed with the love of Christ; so meditate of the Truths of God, as to be transformed into them; and so meditate of sin as to get his heart to hate sin."[4]

Spiritual conversations with other Christians help deepen our relationship with Christ as well. To our detriment we keep private the nature of our spiritual lives. We benefit from having spiritual talks with others we trust and discussing the status of our relationship with Christ and its ups and downs.

YOUR LOVE IS BETTER THAN WINE
As you fill your God space with the Spirit of Christ, entering into his love chamber (Song of Songs 1:4), you may be amazed at how the feeling of emptiness begins to fade away (Song of Songs 4:10).

Charles Spurgeon's sermon on Song of Songs 1:2 begins to explain what it means that Christ's love is better than wine:

I. CHRIST'S LOVE IS BETTER THAN WINE BE-CAUSE OF WHAT IT IS NOT—
because it may be taken without question
because it is to be had without money

because it is to be enjoyed without cloying
because it is without lees
because it will never, as wine will, turn sour
because it produces no ill effects

II. CHRIST'S LOVE IS BETTER THAN WINE BE-
CAUSE OF WHAT IT IS—
it has certain healing properties
it gives strength
it gives joy
it gives sacred exhilaration

As Father Brakel puts it, a deep relationship with
Christ "consists in having fellowship with God, to enjoy His intimate affection, to receive a foretaste of heav-
en, to be changed into His image, to be adorned with the
luster of His glory, and to enjoy all that your soul finds
to delight in. What more could you
wish upon earth?"[5]

> A robust devotional life is not a magic formula to make addictions suddenly disappear.

A robust devotional life is not a
magic formula to make addictions
suddenly disappear. But because
overcoming addiction is first of all a matter of the heart,
your relationship with Christ is a vital component of a
holistic approach to serenity.

If any words are applicable to an addict, they are those
of the fourteenth-century monk Thomas à Kempis in
The Imitation of Christ: "Turn your whole heart toward
God, therefore, and forsake this heartless world. In that

way, you will find rest for your soul. Place no value on external things; pay attention instead to what is within you. You will then see the kingdom of God taking shape within you. This is the kingdom of peace and joy."[6]

In the **third secret** of kicking the habit, you come to discover that only Jesus can fill that hole in your heart. When our hearts are in the right place and the right person is in our hearts—as Ashley discovered, to her delight—it is indeed better than alcohol, drugs, sex or even robbing convenience stores.

So why not make a new start with Jesus today?

KEY IDEAS FROM CHAPTER 3

> Deep within every addict, there is a God space that addictions seek to fill in a counterfeit way.

> Only Jesus can truly fill that void in your heart, and he is knocking on the door.

> Life with Christ can be deepened through Bible study, prayer, singing, meditation and spiritual conversation.

> What the addict most needs to comprehend and experience is that Christ's love is better than wine.

> Those on the journey to serenity must discover a heartfelt relationship with Jesus Christ.

SECRET 4
RENEW YOUR MIND

SECRET 4
R E N E W   Y O U R   M I N D

Do not conform to the pattern of this world, but be transformed by the renewing of your mind.
–Romans 12:2

The story goes that the philosopher René Descartes entered a pub for a beer. When he finished it, the bartender said, "René, do you want another?"

"I think not," replied Descartes. And *poof*, he disappeared.

Okay, so that joke might have gotten past some of you.

Descartes, the famous Enlightenment philosopher, is known for the maxim "I think, therefore I am." He meant that one's ability to reason constitutes the supreme function of human existence. From this philosophy came the belief that with the mind, a person can solve any and all of his or her problems.

STINKING THINKING
We tend to take for granted the fact that people who commit crimes may spend many, many years behind

bars. But for most of human history, this was not the case.

Our current practice of long-term incarceration is based on the bankrupt philosophy of the Enlightenment. Thus, the idea behind lengthy prison terms is that if we give people enough time to think about their crimes, they will magically get better. Solitary confinement takes this belief to an extreme. Theoretically, the person is given an opportunity to think long and hard without any distractions.

Of course, as skyrocketing recidivism rates indicate, nothing could be further from the truth. In fact, if anything, incarceration tends to make people worse rather than better.

That is because addictions thrive on our "stinking thinking," to use a phrase coined by Alcoholics Anonymous. By nature, our minds are thoroughly corrupt and will keep tripping us up unless we experience a complete renewal of the mind through Christ who strengthens us (Philippians 4:13).

President Franklin D. Roosevelt noted, "Men are not prisoners of fate, but prisoners of their own minds." Nothing could be truer of an addict.

> Addictions thrive on stinking thinking.

In light of the failure of Enlightenment philosophy, Martin Luther's earlier comments on human reason have proven all the more true: "Reason is a whore, the greatest enemy that faith has; it never comes to the aid of spiritual things, but more frequently than not struggles against the divine word, treating with contempt all that emanates from God."

AUTOMATIC RECORD AND REPLAY

Experts believe addictions are 90 percent a matter of the mind. Your brain is amazingly complex but easily fooled.

When you experience a pleasurable event, your brain records the experience, and if you do it often enough, your mind physically reshapes itself with neural pathways that drive you to repeat that event.[7]

Let's say you end every day with a few drinks, have a couple of smokes after every meal, or gamble or shop whenever you feel down. Your mind records the sights, sounds and feelings of these rituals. Eventually, neural pathways will be formed in your brain, and they will convince you that each situation requires the accompanying "feel good" behavior.

But the mind can also be reshaped for the better. That is why most successful rehabilitation programs last thirty days. When removed from our normal routines, our minds must recalibrate and adjust to a new environment that lacks the old sights and sounds. The urge for the addicting substance or activity begins to disappear as the brain creates new pathways.

Of course, returning to an old routine can summon the old behavior, which remains stored for a while in your long-term memory. The chances that this old behavior will survive and influence you diminish significantly over time, specifically after two years, five years and seven years. We will return to these milestones later in the book.

"GONNA GET YOUR MIND RIGHT"

For this change of thinking to take place, it is vital not only to clear out the stinking thinking but also to fill the mind with the fragrance of the knowledge of Christ (2 Corinthians 2:14), rehearsing the constant refrain of who we *were* by nature and who we now *are* in Christ by grace.

In the 1967 classic film *Cool Hand Luke*, Paul Newman plays an inmate on a chain gang who has the urge to escape. However, whenever he attempts to do so, he is caught and returned to the compound. Each time, the punishment ordered by the captain is more severe. He tells Luke, "You gonna get your mind right, Luke—and I mean right."

The captain is for the most part successful in ridding the men of the notion to escape. The problem is that their minds are not filled with a substitute for the stinking thinking (from the captain's perspective). So those with "their minds right" are reduced to compliant zombies.

Overcoming addiction requires transformation, and transformation comes from the renewal of your mind (Romans 12:2). Renewing your mind means filling your head with a substitute for the stinking thinking.

Whatever is true,
whatever is noble,
whatever is right,
whatever is pure,
whatever is lovely,
whatever is admirable—
if anything is excellent or praiseworthy—
think about such things.
–Philippians 4:8

It is important not only to nurture a *heartfelt,* personal relationship with Jesus, as we discussed in the last chapter, but also to renew your *mind* with the things of God as revealed in his Holy Word. As people made in his image and renewed in Christ, we are invited to think God's thoughts after him.

COVENANT REMEMBERING

It is by no mistake that a key idea in Scripture is the importance of the act of remembering. The term occurs literally hundreds of times. Here are some examples from the Old and New Testaments:

> ❭ Remember all the commandments of the Lord (Numbers 15:39).

- ❯ Remember the wonders he has done (1 Chronicles 16:12).
- ❯ Remember the words of the Lord Jesus (Acts 20:35).
- ❯ Remember those in prison (Hebrews 13:3).

We refer to this as "covenant," or "biblical," remembering. But what exactly does that mean?

When my daughters were young, one of their hobbies was scrapbooking. From what I recall, they would paste pictures of special events with family and friends into their scrapbooks, scribbling words and drawing decorations around them.

The idea was that from time to time you would take the book of memories out to "remember" the party or outing. Then you would put the book of memories back on the shelf. You wouldn't think much about it until the next time you dusted it off.

That is precisely what covenant remembering is *not!*

Covenant remembering is more like this: Johnny stumbles down the kitchen stairs in the morning. Mom, busy making breakfast, asks, "Johnny, did you remember to make your bed?"

What does Johnny's mom mean by that? Well, she is asking not only if it crossed his mind to make his bed but also if he *actually made it!*

Biblical remembering is bringing to mind in order to act. To remember the commandments of the Lord is to bring them to mind in order to *follow* them (Numbers 15:39). To remember prisoners is to bring them to mind in order to *act* on their behalf (Hebrews 13:3).

In Exodus 2:24, God looked down, saw the suffering of his people in Egypt and *remembered* his covenant with Abraham, Isaac and Jacob. Now,

> Covenant remembering is bringing to mind in order to act.

what does that mean? Does it mean that God had forgotten that his people were down there, and then suddenly one day it occurred to him?

Of course not. God never loses his omniscience. When the Bible says that God remembered his people, it means he brought them to mind in order to act on their behalf. And we read subsequently how, with a mighty hand and an outstretched arm, he delivered his people from slavery.

In a similar way, we are called to remember in order to act. We base our actions upon his Word. In fact, in Scripture, remembering is virtually synonymous with obedience.

This, then, is the heartbeat of renewing the mind:

1. Clear out the stinking thinking.
2. Replace it with right thinking focused on the things of God.

3. Remember to live a life consistent with the things of God.

An addict needs to get his or her mind right, and that, clear and simple, is the **fourth secret** of kicking the habit.

This holistic renewing of the mind can occur only because, by faith in Christ, you are indeed a new creature. As you reshape those neural pathways and fill your head with divine thoughts, the Holy Spirit will change your mind and wrench you free from addiction. Your old way of living will grow strangely dim in the light of his love and grace.

But that brings us to the next component of overcoming addiction, which we will tackle in the next chapter: changing our behavior in a way that complements the renewing of our mind. Then, in chapter 6, we will take some advice, as recalled in a Cherokee legend, from a wise old man.

KEY IDEAS FROM CHAPTER 4

> The bankruptcy of the Enlightenment emphasis on rational thought is evident in the destructive quality of an addict's stinking thinking.

> Addictive behavior reshapes the neural pathways of the mind so that repeating a pleasurable event— even when it is destructive—becomes the path of least resistance.

> People are in desperate need of the renewal of their minds, which occurs as they learn to think God's thoughts.

> Biblical remembering is calling God's Word to mind in order to act on it.

SECRET 5
RUN THE TRIANGLE OFFENSE

SECRET 5

R U N   T H E   T R I A N G L E   O F F E N S E

I press on toward the goal to win the prize for which God has called me heavenward in Christ Jesus.
–Philippians 3:14

Everyone knows that Phil Jackson is the greatest basketball coach of all time. Eleven NBA championships will cement his legacy in the Basketball Hall of Fame forever. The centerpiece of his winning ways was the triangle offense. In this chapter, you will learn how to run another version of the triangle offense—a version designed to achieve victory over addictions.

Jackson's triangle offense was complicated. This one is simple. Also an example of a "feedback loop,"[8] it is a game plan for overcoming addiction by becoming acutely aware of the details of your habit(s). The awareness of this secret breeds champions.

Rather than stumbling in a fog as addictions sweep you along, you take control with scientific precision to observe with absolute clarity exactly what is happening. This secret of clarity is vital for going on the offensive and overcoming your most vicious opponent, denial.

As you run this offense, your consumption can dramatically decline, disappear altogether or come under manageable control. Keep in mind what Confucius once said: "It does not matter how slowly you go so long as you do not stop."

According to Coach Jackson, "The ideal way to win a championship is step by step." Our triangle offense contains three simple steps: record, review and reflect.

STEP 1: RECORD

Every day, keep track of the extent of your involvement in the addiction(s). Count how many drinks or hits you take, how many cigarettes or joints you smoke or how much you gamble or eat. Record these amounts on a scrap of paper you keep with you, type them into your smartphone or keep track in some other way.

At the end of the day, document the totals for each addiction on a calendar or in a diary. If you don't keep a log, you won't remember, or your figures will be imprecise. Then the fog remains and denial wins.

KEEPING A SCORECARD

1	2	3	4	5
12-C 8-B	20-C 6-B	25-C 10-B	10-C 4-B	40-C 12-B

C = cigarettes   B = beers

Think of your record as a golf scorecard—the lower the score, the better. When I first started golfing as a young boy, I purchased a little watch-like tool on which I kept track of all of my strokes—too many to try to count by replaying the strokes in my mind at the end of the game.

When I improved to bogey golf (averaging one over par), I didn't need the watch anymore, but I still wrote down my score. And I didn't cheat! It is important to count *all* the strokes; otherwise you will just be fooling yourself. You don't get any mulligans (do-overs), but don't beat yourself up over a "bad hole," either.

Keep your record confidential so that you have no reason to be dishonest in recording your data. You are wasting your time if you fudge the figures.

STEP 2: REVIEW

John Calvin says that true wisdom consists of two things: knowledge of God and knowledge of self.[9] The next step, perhaps best taken the following morning, will provide knowledge of self when it comes to your addiction.

In the second step of the triangle offense, you review objectively how the last day went and how it compares with previous days.

The best way to conduct this review is to put the data on a graph. If you have access to a computer, a program such as PowerPoint or Microsoft Excel will help you graph the information easily. Graphing the daily stats will enhance your daily debriefing immensely.

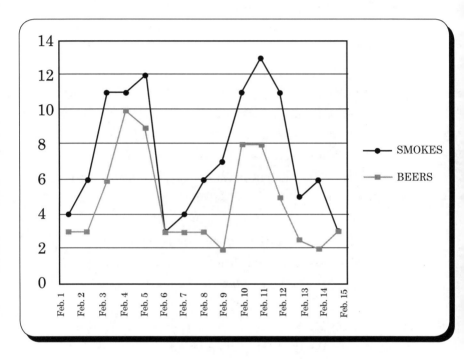

Carefully analyze the data you have collected—and remember, the evidence doesn't lie. Be unbiased and detached, not judgmental or hard on yourself, as you investigate. Do not rationalize the activity. Do not feel guilty about it. Just analyze it as a scientist would.

In your analysis, ask objective questions such as the following:

> How much was consumed?
> Is consumption increasing or decreasing?

> Is there a pattern emerging?
> Are there certain days on which consumption has accelerated or decelerated? Why?
> Do any particular events appear to coincide with fluctuations?

As you analyze the data, you may discover that usage tends to spike on the weekends, when you have more time on your hands. Perhaps it declines on days when you have important evening appointments. Maybe it goes up or down when you are on vacation.

It is likely that you were not fully aware of how much you were consuming on any given day. The graph makes abundantly clear exactly what is happening, but it is up to you to fill in the details and context regarding the data on the chart.

Write down a summary of your analysis.

STEP 3: REFLECT

In the final step, you will reflect on the day and your addiction(s), as well as the history that is accumulating. Consider what might happen if you continue this pattern. Weigh the consequences of your actions. Ponder the possibilities of progress. Do you desire to increase or decrease your involvement the next day?

Consider how to set things in the right direction. Contemplate what to do next. Visualize what the data will look like in your next entry. Meditate on your ultimate source of strength and courage, Christ Jesus.

As you reflect, remember this famous quotation from Shakespeare's *Hamlet*: "To thine own self be true." While Step 1 requires brutal accuracy and Step 2 requires brutal objectivity, Step 3 requires brutal honesty.

Then, with your reflection for the day complete, start again at Step 1 as a new day begins. Keep running the offense daily. If you carefully keep your record, in a few months you will have valuable information about whether your addiction is in decline, under control or in need of more drastic measures.

THE TRIANGLE OFFENSE

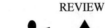

REVIEW

RECORD   REFLECT

REQUIREMENTS OF THE TRIANGLE OFFENSE

Step	Requirement
1. Record	Brutal Accuracy
2. Review	Brutal Objectivity
3. Reflect	Brutal Honesty

AN ADDICT'S GREATEST ENEMY

At this point, I want to let you in on a little secret. As you run the triangle offense, something hideous will rear its ugly head—the greatest enemy to your victory.

An addict's greatest enemy is time. "Normal" folks see time as the enemy when there isn't enough of it. For an addict, however, it is just the opposite. Time is the enemy when there is *too much of it.*

In fact, addicts do not experience time normally until they are engaged in their addictions. Then time flies. But with too much time on their hands, they are suckers for their addictions.

If you examine your chart carefully, one of the things you will likely discover is that you drank or shopped or dabbled in porn more on days or evenings when you had too much time on your hands.

When you have too much time on your hands, your old way of stinking thinking begins to mess with your mind (see chapter 4). Your heart begins to wander (see chapter 3). Time is your strongest opponent, your worst enemy.

That means you need to master your time. Keep busy during free time when you are most vulnerable. Fill your time with productive activity.

Schedule meetings that do not allow you to consume.

Join a Bible study. Schedule activities with your kids. Read a book. Attend AA. Detail your car. Clean the house. Take up new hobbies. Get a second job. Hang out with people who do not consume rather than with those who do.

Never forget: an addiction will always find a way to fill the time allotted (or allowed) for it.

> "Time is the cruelest teacher; first she gives the test, then teaches the lesson." –Leonard Bernstein

There is a reason it is said that idle hands are the devil's playground. Instead of being idle, we are to redeem the time because the days are evil (Ephesians 5:16). We are to make the most of our time.

Your life does not have to become time poorly spent on addictions. That cannot happen if there is no time for it to occur. Let your chart alert you to when you tend to be most vulnerable. The graph never lies.

Indeed, you can make your greatest advancements— and you can win—if, like a great athlete, you don't waste the clock. Your chart will tell you exactly when you are throwing away the game.

So...study it. Plan ahead. Take evasive action.

By doing this, you will be in charge of your time. When this happens, time will become your closest ally rather than your fiercest enemy, because you will be accomplishing so much for Christ and the advancement of his kingdom rather than living as a pathetic slave to your addiction.

WHY FEEDBACK LOOPS WORK

Surely upon occasion you have seen a large Your Speed sign along the road. Equipped with radar, this sign posts the speed of your automobile as you approach. Even though there are no police present, no tickets issued and no fines assessed, traffic will slow notably in that area of the road, even after the sign is removed. That change is the result of a feedback loop.

Likewise, the Netherlands tested an alternative to taxing cars, licenses and fuel in an attempt to relieve gridlock. The experiment involved equipping each car with a meter, similar to the ones found in taxis, that tracked how many miles had been driven.

Individuals were taxed based on the number of miles they drove, rather than everyone being taxed the same regardless of car and road usage. Here's the kicker: even though the tax collected under the new meter system was less for the average driver, people participating in the experiment drove significantly *less* and used public transportation *more*. This, of course, is the result of another feedback loop in action.

If feedback loops work among the general population, how much more should they work among the faith-based population, especially when it comes to vital life issues?

The triangle offense works because it helps you clearly see and monitor your behavior. Take heart: you are made in the image of God (Genesis 1:27). In Christ, you are experiencing the renewal of your mind (Romans 12:2).

The apostle Paul is recommending a feedback loop when he says explicitly, "Examine yourselves." And why does self-examination work? It is because "Christ Jesus is in you" (2 Corinthians 13:5). Therefore, you *can* change your behavior as you clear the haze that inevitably creeps in with denial.

The **fifth secret** for kicking the habit is coming to clarity on the journey to serenity by discovering that a believer can be *self-correcting*. And that is why the triangle offense is a winning strategy.

> A believer can be self-correcting.

Never forget that you are a new creature; you are more than a champion in him who loves you (Romans 8:37). Someday, you too will be in the hall of fame (Hebrews 11).

KEY IDEAS FROM CHAPTER 5

> The triangle offense (record, review, reflect) is a daily three-step program to bring an addict to clarity, which is a vital secret on the road to sobriety.

> True wisdom consists of knowledge of God and knowledge of self.

> Step 1 of the triangle offense requires brutal accuracy. Step 2 requires brutal objectivity. Step 3 requires brutal honesty.

> An addict's greatest enemy is time.

> Feedback loops work because Christians can and should be self-correcting.

SECRET 6
DON'T FEED THE BAD DOG

SECRET 6

DON'T FEED THE BAD DOG

*For I do not do the good I want to do, but the evil I do
not want to do—this I keep on doing.*
–Romans 7:19

An ancient Cherokee legend recounts a conversation
between a wise old man and his grandson. The old
man, the legend holds, explained to the boy, "Inside of
me, and inside of every person, a terrible fight ensues
between two dogs. One is evil; the other is good. They
fight all the time."

The little boy carefully considered his grandfather's
words. Then, peering up at the wise old man, he asked,
"Which one wins?"

His grandfather smiled and replied simply, "The one I
feed."

The boy paused for a moment and then inquired,
"Which one do you feed, Grandpa?"

The old man looked down at the little boy. "I don't feed
the bad dog anymore," he said softly.

The sixth secret of kicking the habit has to do with starving the bad dog.

STOP IT!

The apostle Paul said something similar when he wrote that each of us has an old self and a new self (Ephesians 4:22–24; Colossians 3:9–11). Scripture uses the language of "putting on" the new self and "putting off" the old self.

This is a metaphor of clothing. You take off the dirty clothes and put on the clean ones. The old clothes represent our old, sinful nature. The new clothes represent our new nature in Christ. And addictions, of course, are part of that filthy old wardrobe.

It is often comfortable to wear the worn-out clothes. They are familiar to you. You have had them for a long time. Perhaps you even have some good memories wearing those old clothes.

But you look a mess.

Thankfully, in Christ you have a brand-new wardrobe—and don't you look good! Tear off the old clothes and throw them in the garbage, once and for all.

In fact, Paul uses even stronger language than that of taking off and putting on clothing. He says to "put to death" the old nature (Colossians 3:5) and, consequently, to bring to life the new nature in Christ. This is akin to starving the mean dog. Get out your shotgun. Take that old mutt out back and put it out of its misery. Then bury it.

Famous comedian and actor Bob Newhart once guest-starred in a MADtv sketch. He portrayed a psychologist who charged only five dollars a session (he would take cash or a check but would not make change). Each session took less than five minutes.

A woman came to him seeking treatment for her claustrophobia, confessing, "I have this fear of being buried alive in a box. In fact, I'm afraid of driving through a tunnel or taking an elevator."

Newhart said that he had just two words for her. He leaned across his desk and yelled, "STOP IT!"

"What do you mean?" the startled woman responded.

He spelled it out for her. "S-T-O-P. New word. I-T. Just... STOP IT!"

The sketch is, of course, humorous. But do you see the truth there as well?

Now we see the pattern:

> Don't feed the bad dog.
> Take off the dirty clothes.
> STOP IT!

EXERCISING CHRIST'S POWER

In addition to following those instructions, we need to feed the good dog, put on the new clothes and start doing the right things.

For example, instead of peeking at porn, read good novels. Instead of doing drugs, take up exercise. Instead of plunking coins into one-armed bandits, donate to a worthy cause.

And then vow never to feed the mean dog again—and to keep feeding the good one. For when you indulge, even a little, in your addiction, you are feeding the wrong dog. That bad dog likes your addiction better than rare steak. If you throw him a bone, he is more than ready to fight and devour the good dog. The secret for victory is that you must stop feeding the bad dog.

Stop feeding him, and he loses his strength. Feed the good dog, and *he* will grow stronger and stronger.

No one can put off the old self and put on the new self for you. But the good news is that you do not have to try to do it in your own strength! Remember where you've been. You have a personal relationship with Jesus Christ and are renewing your mind through the Word.

Alone, you cannot fight off the bad dog. With the Holy Spirit,

> The good news is that you do not have to try this in your own strength.

however, you can do all things through Christ who gives you strength (Philippians 4:13). Overcoming addiction is a matter of the heart, head and hands—but it is not so much an exercise of willpower as it is an exercise of Christ's power.

Once, after sharing these ideas, I received a letter from a student of mine that read, "Dr. Schuringa, I have stopped feeding the bad dog for two days now!"

He's off and running! As Alcoholics Anonymous advises, take it one day at a time.

SUPPORT GROUPS
Members of Alcoholics Anonymous state that their primary purpose is "to stay sober and help other alcoholics to achieve sobriety." Bill Wilson and Dr. Bob Smith (or Bill W. and Dr. Bob) founded the movement in 1935 in Akron, Ohio.

Millions have found meetings of Alcoholics Anonymous (or offshoots such as Narcotics Anonymous, Gamblers Anonymous and so on) helpful as a source of continuing education and support while starving the bad dog. As the name implies, when you attend these meetings, you do so anonymously, using only your first name.

You have to find a meeting that is right for you. At that meeting, there will be discussion and sharing by fellow addicts. You don't have to talk if you don't want to.

They will be discussing topics such as stinking thinking, getting your mind right, celebrating milestones and the like. You can seek advice on whether you need medical help to stay on track.

AA is known for its twelve-step program. Working through these steps during and in between the meetings helps participants keep their addictions at bay while recovering from the damage addiction has inflicted on them and those around them. (For more information on the Twelve Steps, see appendix 3.)

You will also find unconditional acceptance rather than condemnation, even if you stumble along the way and happen to feed the wrong dog.

> Working through these steps helps participants keep their addictions at bay.

It is not unusual to attend several meetings each week during the first weeks of recovery. This can gradually be cut back to just one or two a week. Some folks continue to attend meetings the rest of their lives. Others taper off after reaching critical milestones.

Participants at these meetings will include those who have been "on the wagon" for years and those who have just recently come on board. That is why this is not just any small accountability group—you cannot fool the folks in an AA meeting, and they call a spade a spade. There is more than one way to understand the Scripture that tells us not to neglect meeting together as some have done (Hebrews 10:25). For most addicts, a support group is a lifeline.

Some Christians are bothered by the fact that AA speaks of "a higher power" and "God as you understand Him" rather than affirming the personal God of the Bible in Jesus Christ. As a result, Christian AA groups have started with a degree of success. Most Christians who attend AA groups simply say that the God of the Bible in Christ Jesus is their higher power and is indeed God as they understand him.

At AA, you can also find a sponsor. A sponsor is someone with a number of years of sobriety behind him or her, someone who can mentor you. You can call this person when you are tempted to feed the bad dog.

Refusing to feed the bad dog is the **sixth secret** for kicking the habit. In the next chapter, we will learn the final secret and put all these secrets together to devise a massive plan of attack against the addiction. We will call it "planning for D-Day."

THE SERENITY PRAYER
"God, grant me the serenity to accept the things I cannot change, the courage to change the things I can and wisdom to know the difference."

KEY IDEAS FROM CHAPTER 6

> The heart of breaking an addiction is revealed in the sixth secret of kicking the habit: do not feed the bad dog anymore.

> We replace bad habits with good habits not through willpower but through the exercise of Christ's power.

> For help feeding the right dog, many turn to accountability groups such as those provided by Alcoholics Anonymous.

> Those who are able to stop feeding the bad dog completely have conquered their addiction and have no need to read further!

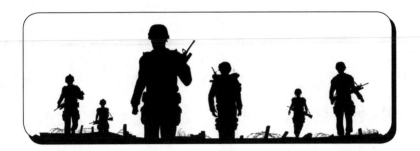

SECRET 7
PLAN FOR D-DAY

SECRET 7

P L A N   F O R   D - D A Y

...choose for yourselves this day whom you will serve...
—Joshua 24:15

The term "D-Day" has become synonymous with June 6, 1944, a date indelibly marked on the minds of the Greatest Generation. On that day, Allied forces landed on the beaches of Normandy to free Europe from Nazi domination.

Considered one of the largest amphibious assaults in history, D-Day was carefully and extensively planned. There could be no room for error. Millions of lives depended on it.

Because the operation was highly successful, France was liberated in three months and all of Europe was secured by spring. That Normandy landing, D-Day, is considered the beginning of the end of World War II.

The term "D-Day" is routinely used in the military to recall June 6, and it is also used to denote the day any major operation or event will take place. But its use is not limited to the military. It can refer to "any day of special significance, as one marking an important event or goal."[10] It is especially relevant when referring to "the day on which any large-scale operation is planned to start."[11]

While "D-Day" can refer to many things, it does seem best reserved for something that is a big deal. I would not refer to my next day's plan to have my oil changed as "D-Day."

We could define "D-Day" as "a day of special significance on which to launch a major, life-changing initiative, one that requires extensive planning, a large-scale operation and a clearly defined strategic goal to accomplish."

For several months or perhaps more than a year, you have been running the triangle offense. You have been graphing a visual record of your performance and using what is often called a "feedback loop."

You then learned the sixth secret, that is, that to kick your habit you will need to feed the good dog and starve the bad dog.

Now is the time to take all the secrets learned up to this point and put them into action.

To do so, you will need to make a plan and set a D-Day,

a day when you will storm the beaches and launch the initiative.

Is the day of quitting your habit weighty enough to be called "D-Day"? Well, let's go back to our above definition. The day you decide to completely quit something such as booze, smoking or drugs certainly is

> a day of special significance,
> the launch of a major, life-changing initiative,
> something that requires extensive planning in order to be successful,
> a large-scale operation (affecting virtually every area of your life) and
> possible with a clearly defined strategic goal to accomplish.

In fact, overcoming addiction before it overcomes you is a war you are fighting. Addictions take no prisoners. They will seduce you, drive you insane and, finally, kill you. Literally. You may have lost a few battles, but you do not need to lose the war. In order to be victorious, you need a D-Day and an entire strategy to win the assault after you land on the beach. Your D-Day can be (1) self-imposed, (2) accomplished with the help of rehab or (3) initiated by an intervention.

> To overcome an addiction, you have to wage a war.

SELF-IMPOSED D-DAY
First of all, you need to set a date. Why? Because everything in you wants to keep using. With

time to focus on your D-Day, however, you will be more likely to actually take the leap and quit. It takes more time than we think to break our wills. Consider the old saying "A person convinced against his will is of the same opinion still."

You may think that you are resolved to quit, but in actuality the addiction is smarter than you think. As an addict, you will gladly agree to quitting *tomorrow*.

However, if you have time daily—and several times a day—to resolve to quit on a particular date you have set, the relentless pounding of that decision into your mind can outsmart the addiction.

How far out should you plan your D-Day? That is up to you. I would suggest one to three months. That sounds like a long time, but the longer the better—unless your addiction is doing immediate harm—so that you have more time to "brainwash" yourself into actually quitting.

If at all possible, choose a day that is the first of several when you plan to be removed from your ordinary routine, such as when you are on a family vacation or a missions trip.

Why? As discussed in chapter 4, changing locations fools your brain, which no longer has access to the customary surroundings that the addiction has learned to savor.

Just as the D-Day of 1944 was a surprise assault on the enemy, so too your D-Day will be a surprise assault on the addiction. The part of your brain that the addiction controls will not have foreseen the attack and will not have had the opportunity to adjust its neural pathways.

Preparing to storm the beach also involves medical preparations. By now, you should be sure that you are eating well and, especially, that you are on a vitamin regimen.

Alcohol and drug usage, for example, affect the metabolism of nutrients and vitamins that are important for your body. Alcoholics tend to be low on vitamins B and C because the alcohol prevents full metabolism of these and other vitamins. A super-dose of an adult multivitamin will probably do the trick.

Having adequate vitamins and nutrients helps in the withdrawal process by lessening withdrawal symptoms. Your body will draw strength from the vitamins as they begin to metabolize at full strength.

You may think that vitamins and nutrients are only necessary for the successful withdrawal from addictions that involve ingested substances. Not so. You should assume that any addiction will have negative effects upon your body, its metabolism and your overall health.

Second, it would be wise to confer with your physician, inviting him or her to help you plan for D-Day. At the very least, your doctor can advise you on your vitamin intake. For some addicts, doctors may prescribe a temporary medication to ease withdrawal during the first week or two. Your doctor may also recommend an accompanying diet and exercise regimen.

At last, your D-Day will arrive, and it will come time to hit the beach, strike the enemy and take back your territory.

It would be wise to invite your physician to help you.

Not drinking today does not mean that you will not drink tomorrow. However, when you get one day under your belt, you may be surprised how motivated you are to go after another. Jesus has the best advice for D-Day and each day after that: "Therefore do not worry about tomorrow, for tomorrow will worry about itself" (Matthew 6:34).

Think of each day as getting back another piece of the territory that your addiction occupied.

Yes, your body will go through withdrawal, regardless of the addiction. However, detoxification will be somewhat different for each person. It takes a couple of days for the alcohol or drugs to get out of your system, but some have said that the fifth day is the worst.[12]

Every day, you are winning a battle. It takes time to win the war—first two weeks and then thirty days before the initial assault is successful.

You will not be going through it alone. Your morning and evening devotions and relationship with Jesus (see chapter 3) will grow more precious than you ever imagined. He will be taking the journey with you. He will be a source of incredible strength over the evil one, who is present in your addiction. Remember, all power on heaven and earth has been given to Jesus (Matthew 28:18). And he will share that power with you because he is in you (Romans 8:11).

D-DAY WITH THE HELP OF REHAB

It is possible that your self-imposed D-Day was not as successful as you had hoped. It is okay to try it more than once. But if you fail, you can plan a D-Day with a little more help—rehab.

Rehab has all the main ingredients to help you succeed. Rehabilitation programs last anywhere from two weeks to nine months. I recommend a program of thirty days or more. Experts agree that it takes thirty days to make a habit and thirty days to break a habit.

Away from the circumstances of your addiction—in a facility where the neural pathways of your brain will be fooled by the strange environment—you will receive the medical, psychological and spiritual assistance you need to get free.

Just be sure to see the program through to the end.

I once interviewed Michael Lohan, father of troubled

starlet Lindsay Lohan, on my radio program, *Crossroad Connection*. Having conquered addictions himself, he knows what it takes, especially with the rich and famous.

One problem, he said, is that celebrities check themselves into rehab and then bail after a few days or a couple of weeks, having changed their minds or thinking they are on top of it.

So Michael told me he was developing a celebrity rehab program on a yacht out on the ocean. Why? To provide a comfortable atmosphere for the rich and famous? No. Without booze or drugs on board, it would not be a party boat. The yacht would be at sea so that the celebrity clients couldn't bail. Michael would make sure they were far enough out to sea that they could not swim to shore—let alone fend off the sharks.

The day you enter rehab will be your D-Day, the day when you storm the beach, win back conquered territory and triumph over your addiction at last.

D-DAY THROUGH INTERVENTION
Your loved ones may also determine your D-Day. Bob knew deep down that he was in trouble, but he was also deep in denial. He got up late and hadn't started drinking yet when a number of cars pulled up in the driveway.

People—including his boss, his best friend, two of his

adult children, his wife, his neighbor and a stranger he didn't know—filed into the house.

"What the heck is going on here?" he growled as he stumbled into the family room where everyone had taken a seat.

"Hi," said the stranger. "My name is Dan. Please, Bob, take a seat for a few minutes." Reluctantly, Bob took a seat in his easy chair, which they had reserved for him.

"Bob," his wife, Martha, began, "you know how much I love you, how much we all love you, but we are deeply worried about you. We want to talk with you about the effect your drinking is having on your life, and ours."

One by one, in a totally objective manner, each person present cataloged concrete, detailed examples of how Bob's drinking had caused problems. Without judging or moralizing, they simply recited the facts.

Bob's boss listed by date some of the many days Bob had been late coming to work because of his drinking. His best friend recalled specific times he had had to drive Bob home from various activities. His kids recalled the times (and dates) when he had stumbled into the house in the middle of the night, as well as the bruises they had found on their mother. And his wife, well, she had a story or two of her own to tell.

At the end of the time of sharing, Dan, the facilitator,

asked Bob if any of the information was inaccurate. "No," he responded. "It's all true. Can't deny it."

"Well then, you know deep down that your life is out of control," said Dan.

"Because we care for you," he continued, "we have a room in an excellent rehab center reserved just for you. It's waiting. They have professionals there and a program that can help put this nightmare behind you, once and for all. Your bag is already packed, and we want to take you there right now."

> "Because we care for you, we have a room in an excellent rehab center reserved just for you."

What you just witnessed was an intervention. As you can see, in an intervention, family and friends gently—but honestly and firmly—confront their loved one about his or her addiction. The goal is for the subject of the intervention to respond positively at that moment and to get into the car to go to a rehab center. I have seen it happen many times. But it does not always work according to plan.

I remember leading the intervention for my dad—not an easy thing to do. At the end of our time of sharing, he did not go to rehab. In fact, he got up and left the room.

However, Dad now admits that after facing his entire family in such a painful but loving way, drinking was no longer an option for him. He checked himself into rehab a month later and has not had a drink since. Should you have people around you who care enough to perform an intervention, don't resist. Go to rehab and become a new person.

MILESTONES

Though you must take it one day at a time, here is an elaboration on the milestones to work toward as you move through the seven secrets of kicking your habits. As you pass each milestone, you will enter more deeply into that journey of serenity and experience the "already" of the bliss we share in Christ Jesus.

Thirty Days: The first thirty days are crucial. If you can get through the first thirty days, you will be well on your way to conquering your addiction. Why are those thirty days so important? Well, recall that it takes thirty days to make a habit and thirty days to break a habit. Anything you do for a month straight becomes part of you. That is why the first month is so important for the "put off" and "put on" strategy. After thirty days, you are halfway there.

Two Years: When you pass the two-year mark, you are 75 percent "cured" of your addiction. A nice place to be! This is a critical milestone in recovery.

Five Years: When you have refused to feed the bad dog for five years, you will be 90 percent freed from your addiction.

Seven Years: After seven years of freedom, you will be 100 percent cured and no more likely to be enslaved by your addiction than someone who has never been hooked.

PERCENT CHANCE OF SUCCESS

KEY IDEAS FROM CHAPTER 7

> D-Day for conquering your addiction can be self-imposed, accompanied by rehab or initiated through an intervention.

> Your physician can provide you with important information regarding your current health and provide recommendations for anticipated needs.

> Rehab may provide the best circumstances and holistic support for your D-Day.

> People who love the addict may conduct an intervention to convince him or her to enter treatment.

> While taking one day at a time, you can look forward to milestones on your journey.

MAKE THE JOURNEY
Y O U R   D E S T I N A T I O N

People of faith think about the afterlife, about heaven. You might have heard the phrase "He's so heavenly minded, he's no earthly good." Life on this earth is incomparably short next to eternity, so it may indeed be tempting to focus on the next life to the neglect of this one.

An addict is "heavenly minded" in that he or she is seeking to escape from this world to a counterfeit heaven. But in this way, an addict is like the person napping on the tour bus as it passes the Grand Canyon! The fact is that even addicts can be so heavenly minded that they are no earthly good!

You may find the prospect of putting the seven secrets to work and experiencing life head on a bit frightening. And that is understandable: your addiction has buffered life's hurts and disappointments to a certain extent for perhaps a very long time.

There is a great story about Johnny Cash and his wife, June Carter Cash, entertaining Bono for dinner in their home. It is said that, as was Cash's custom, he prayed to begin the meal. At the end of the prayer, with head still bowed, he peered up at Bono and said, "Sure do miss the drugs, though."

Saying goodbye to your addiction is like parting with an old friend. But it was not a real friend, because it was dragging you down! Johnny Cash's final album, produced by Rick Rubin and released after Cash's death, was arguably the best of his entire career. His final victory over drugs after a lifelong struggle ushered him into a new and wondrous world.

Johnny learned the secrets. And so can you.

STUDY GUIDE

CHAPTER 1

1. Describe the three components of an addiction.

    A.

    B.

    C.

2. On this basis, list the addictions you have.

3. In what ways are all addictions alike?

4. Describe the difference between a drunkard and an alcoholic.

5. List habits you have that could become addictions.

6. Why do you think you might be an addict?

7. Take the MAST Test in appendix 2, tailoring it to your addiction(s). How did you score? Do you think you might be an addict regardless of what the score says?

8. In what concrete ways have addictions negatively affected your life?

9. Is it obvious to others that you have a problem, or are you at this point still a highly functioning addict?

10. Denial ain't no _____ in _____.

11. The **first secret** for kicking the habit is _____ that you _____ a _____.

CHAPTER 2

1. In what ways is addiction a sin?

2. In what ways is addiction a disease?

3. What would you say to Dr. Will Powers?

4. What would you say to Dr. Kent Helpit?

5. Which of your addictions are sinful and need to be quit completely?

6. Which of your addictions are not necessarily sinful in and of themselves but need to be brought under control?

7. This book advocates a holistic approach. Why do you think it is important to treat the whole person?

8. The **second secret** for kicking the habit is that the _____ and _____ schools happen to be two _____ of the same _____.

CHAPTER 3

1. Describe in your own words how your addiction makes you feel "better."

2. Can you think of any events in your life that might have contributed to the hole in your heart? Childhood emotional, physical or sexual abuse? An absent father?

3. How long have you been a Christian? Describe when and how it happened.

4. What do you think it would feel like for Jesus to be knocking on the door of your heart in order to have a deeper relationship with you? Is he inviting you to answer the door right now?

5. List four ways you could deepen your relationship with Christ.

   A.

   B.

   C.

   D.

6. List and memorize three ways Christ's love is better than your addiction.

   A.

   B.

   C.

7. The **third secret** for kicking the habit is coming to realize that only _____ can _____ that _____ in your _____.

CHAPTER 4

1. What is "stinking thinking," and how does it get in the way of overcoming addictions?

2. According to Martin Luther, "Reason is a _____ and the greatest _____ that faith has."

3. Describe in your own words what effect your addiction and the circumstances of indulging in your addiction have had on your brain. Give a specific example from your own life.

4. What concrete steps can you take to reverse this damage?

5. Write down and memorize Romans 12:2.

6. What is "covenant remembering"?

7. The **fourth secret** for kicking the habit is to
_____ your mind.

CHAPTER 5

1. The triangle offense is a strategy that contains three
simple steps: _____, _____ and
_____.

2. List the addiction(s) against which you could run the
triangle offense.

3. How will you record your usage? (Will you use a scrap

of paper, smartphone, voice recorder, journal or something else?)

4. Do you desire to *quit* or *control* your addiction with the triangle offense? Why?

5. What kind of information will your graph provide you?

6. An addict's greatest enemy is _____.

7. Use Scripture to show why feedback loops such as the triangle offense work for believers.

8. The **fifth secret** for kicking the habit is that a believer is _____-_____.

1. The **sixth secret** for overcoming an addiction is to _____ feeding the bad _____.

2. Describe the ways in which you feed the bad dog.

3. Read and summarize in your own words Ephesians 4:22–24 and Colossians 3:9–11.

4. Describe why it is important for kicking the habit to be about exercising Christ's power rather than your own willpower.

5. For each of the twelve steps (see appendix 3), write a sentence or two that describes where you are right now.

A.

B.

C.

D.

E.

F.

G.

H.

I.

J.

K.

L.

6. Research and write down the time and place of an AA meeting or similar support group that you can attend.

7. Commit to praying the Serenity Prayer once a day.

CHAPTER 7

1. The **seventh secret** for overcoming addiction is to _____ for D-Day.

2. List the three ways your D-Day can take place.

A.

B.

C.

3. Why is it important to set a date for a self-imposed D-Day?

4. Write down the name of your primary care physician and the last time you had a complete physical.

5. Would you feel comfortable sharing the details of your addiction with your physician? Why or why not?

6. What can checking yourself into rehab do for you?

7. Research rehabilitation centers in your area where you could check in if necessary. (Also check to see which programs your health insurance would cover.)

8. Describe in your own words what an intervention is. Do you think you would be open to an intervention?

9. Do you have a sense that you have been missing out on life because of your addiction? Describe two specific ways in which you think that is true.

   A.

   B.

10. Picture what you and your life will look like after each milestone.

    30 days:

2 years:

5 years:

7 years:

11. Read appendix 4 on how addictions affect the family. Can you see any of these roles in your family or in the family you grew up with? List them below.

THE MAST TEST

The MAST Test is a simple, self-scoring test that helps assess if you have a drinking problem.

Please answer YES or NO to the following questions:

1. Do you feel you are a normal drinker? ("Normal" is ` defined as drinking as much or less than most other people.)
   YES or NO

2. Have you ever awakened the morning after some drinking the night before and found that you could not remember a part of the evening?
   YES or NO

3. Does any near relative or close friend ever worry or complain about your drinking?
   YES or NO

4. Can you stop drinking without difficulty after one or two drinks?
   YES or NO

5. Do you ever feel guilty about your drinking?
   YES or NO

6. Have you ever attended a meeting of Alcoholics Anonymous (AA)?
YES or NO

7. Have you ever gotten into physical fights when drinking?
YES or NO

8. Has drinking ever created problems between you and a near relative or close friend?
YES or NO

9. Has any family member or close friend gone to anyone for help about your drinking?
YES or NO

10. Have you ever lost friends because of your drinking?
YES or NO

11. Have you ever gotten into trouble at work because of drinking?
YES or NO

12. Have you ever lost a job because of drinking?
YES or NO

13. Have you ever neglected your obligations, your family or your work for two or more days in a row because you were drinking?
YES or NO

14. Do you drink before noon fairly often?
    YES or NO

15. Have you ever been told you have liver trouble such
    as cirrhosis?
    YES or NO

16. After heavy drinking, have you ever had delirium
    tremens (DTs), severe shaking or visual or auditory
    (hearing) hallucinations?
    YES or NO

17. Have you ever gone to anyone for help about your
    drinking?
    YES or NO

18. Have you ever been hospitalized because of
    drinking?
    YES or NO

19. Has your drinking ever resulted in your being
    hospitalized in a psychiatric ward?
    YES or NO

20. Have you ever gone to any doctor, social worker,
    clergyman or mental health clinic for help with any
    emotional problem in which drinking was part of
    the problem?
    YES or NO

21. Have you been arrested more than once for driving under the influence of alcohol?
    YES or NO

22. Have you ever been arrested, even for a few hours, because of other behavior while drinking?
    (If yes, how many times? _____)
    YES or NO

SCORING

Please score one point if you answered the following:
1: NO
2: YES
3: YES
4: NO
5–22: YES

Add up the points and compare with the following scorecard:
0–2: No apparent problem
3–5: Early or middle problem drinker
6 or more: Problem drinker

THE TWELVE STEPS

Step 1: We admitted we were powerless over our addiction—that our lives had become unmanageable.

Step 2: Came to believe that a Power greater than ourselves could restore us to sanity.

Step 3: Made a decision to turn our will and our lives over to the care of God *as we understood Him.*

Step 4: Made a searching and fearless moral inventory of ourselves.

Step 5: Admitted to God, to ourselves and to another human being the exact nature of our wrongs.

Step 6: Were entirely ready to have God remove all these defects of character.

Step 7: Humbly asked Him to remove our shortcomings.

Step 8: Made a list of all persons we had harmed, and became willing to make amends to them all.

Step 9:   Made direct amends to such people wherever possible, except when to do so would injure them or others.

Step 10:   Continued to take personal inventory and when we were wrong promptly admitted it.

Step 11:   Sought through prayer and meditation to improve our conscious contact with God, *as we understood Him,* praying only for knowledge of His will for us and the power to carry that out.

Step 12:   Having had a spiritual awakening as the result of these steps, we tried to carry this message to other addicts, and to practice these principles in all our affairs.[13]

EFFECTS OF ADDICTION ON THE FAMILY

When there is an addict in the family, it affects the entire family so that what was perhaps functioning rather well becomes dysfunctional. In a dysfunctional family, various members take on one or more of the following roles (which can change).

THE ENABLER

Usually, the spouse, in one way or another, enables the addict to continue the behavior. Oddly enough, this is most often accomplished by seeking to control the addict's consumption and behavior rather than letting the addiction play itself out.

THE RESPONSIBLE CHILD

One of the children, often the oldest, takes responsibility for the behavior of the addict. For example, this is the child who puts a blanket on the drunken mother passed out on the couch and makes sure the rest of the kids get some supper.

THE GOLDEN CHILD

The golden child is the family favorite who can do no wrong. This child works very hard to be liked by everyone and to please everyone. (This person can also be the clown; see below.)

THE SCAPEGOAT
Unfortunately, in a dysfunctional family, one of its members tends to "act out" the problems of the family. This child may have problems in school, initiate problems in the home or perhaps have brushes with the law. It would not be unusual for this child to also have addiction problems.

THE HIDDEN CHILD
When the lamps are flying and all hell breaks loose, this child runs for cover. Perhaps during a blowout, he or she will hide in the closet. This child spends a lot of time alone in the bedroom, reading, watching TV or using Facebook and just wants to stay out of the fray until it blows over.

THE CLOWN
In the midst of the doom and gloom, this child is the comedian. He or she can keep the family laughing though times are desperate. The clown can always put a smile on Mom's face.

While it is true that all family members, even in fully functional families, tend to take on various roles such as the ones above, these roles are dangerously exaggerated in a dysfunctional family so that not only the addict but every family member is very sick.

That is why it is recommended that the entire family get help and seek out a support group such as Al-Anon or Alateen.

The good news is that as you get better, so will your family! Of course, there may be some irreversible damage (the scapegoat lands in prison, the hidden child runs away or the divorce is already in progress), but positive changes will develop over time if you experience victory over your addiction.

In fact, you will discover and enjoy your family in ways you never could have imagined.

1. *Dictionary.com Unabridged*, s.v. "habit," accessed March 26, 2013, http://www.dictionary.com/browse/habit.

2. *Wikipedia*, s.v. "denial," last modified March 26, 2013, http://en.wikipedia.org/wiki/Denial.

3. "Nouthetic" is from a Greek word meaning "to warn or to admonish" and was coined by Jay Adams, who, following the work of O. Hobard Mowrer, rejected the medical model in particular and psychology in general as legitimate fields of research and study. See Jay E. Adams, *Competent to Counsel* (Phillipsburg, NJ: Presbyterian and Reformed Publishing Co., 1978), xvi–xvii.

4. Edmund Calamy, *The Art of Divine Meditation* (London: for Tho. Parkhurst, 1634), 26–28.

5. Wilhelmus à Brakel, *The Christian's Reasonable Service,* vol. 4, trans. Bartel Elshout (Morgan, PA: Soli Deo Gloria Publications, 1995), 30.

6. Thomas à Kempis, *The Imitation of Christ,* trans. P. G. Zomberg (Rockland, ME: Dunstan Press, 1984), 53.

7. For more information on this subject, see Gerald G. May, *Addiction and Grace* (San Francisco: HarperSanFrancisco, 1988).

8. For an explanation of the theological foundation for this approach, see my "Hearing the Word in a Visual Age" (PhD diss., Theologische Universiteit de Kampen, 1995), 10–20. This is summarized in "Wagging the Dog: The Church's Crying Need for Practical Theology," *Calvin Theological Journal* 35 (2000): 151–161.

9. John Calvin, *Institutes of the Christian Religion,* vol. 1, trans. Ford Lewis Battles, Library of Christian Classics 20 (Philadelphia: Westminster Press, 1975), 1.1.1–3, 35–47.

10. *Dictionary.com Unabridged,* s.v. "D-Day," accessed March 27, 2013, http://dictionary.reference.com/browse/d-day?s=t.

11. *Collins English Dictionary – Complete & Unabridged 10th Edition*, s.v. "D-Day," accessed March 27, 2013 http://dictionary.reference.com/browse/d-day?s=t.

12. A small percentage of addicts (likely those involved in their addiction almost 24/7) may have such severe withdrawals as to require medical attention. They may require someone to watch over them for the first week and to call 911 if it appears that life-threatening symptoms are occurring.

13. Alcoholics Anonymous World Services, "The Twelve Steps of Alcoholics Anonymous," May 9, 2002, accessed April 22, 2013, http://www.aa.org/en_pdfs/smf-121_en.pdf.